The "Hush-Hush" Factory

The Story of the Nuffield Mechanisation and Aero Shadow Factory at Tubney Wood, Oxfordshire 1940 -1992

First produced in the early nineties, the history of the Tubney Woods Hush-Hush Factory in Oxfordshire continues to be of local interest.

Now in 2014 this update on the original contains some new information received over the intervening years.

Bofors Gun at the ready

INTRODUCTION

This publication is the result of my investigations into a little-known, but historically significant, example of specialist manufacturing support for the World War 2 war machine.

Only two factories were producing the vital BOFORS gun barrels in Great Britain during this time and this carefully concealed site's buildings remained until 1992.

Unfortunately, it was not possible to preserve the site in its WW2 form as a tribute to the many people who contributed behind the scenes in the Allied victory.

You will read of the conditions under which the factory personnel worked, many of these being young girls performing operations completely alien to them initially - yet Tubney Wood barrels were often described as 'the best'.
This is an interesting and valuable story, having talked to people who worked there in those dark days.

The majority of photographs were taken by myself just prior to the site being demolished, but are accompanied by some unique wartime photographs of some of the workers and two amazing shots of the inside of No.1 machine shop. These two officially taken pictures are the only known ones of the inside of the buildings and showing the workers at work.

After reading the following pages, the next time you pass the entrance at the northern end of the A338 Wantage Road, you will now know more about what went on amongst the pine trees all those years ago.

N J Dawe

The Viscount Lord Nuffield, otherwise known as William Morris, founder and owner of the Cowley car factory at the start, and soon acquiring other companies to add to his empire in the 1920s and 30s all eventually coming under the umbrella of the Nuffield Organisation.

The origins of the Nuffield Organisation started back in the 1890s when Bill Morris, as a young lad of 16 began to build and repair bicycles in a shed in the back of the family home in James Street, Oxford just off the Iffley Road.

Part One
Coventry to Tubney Wood

The British-built Bofors Gun

In 1937, Lord Nuffield, as honorary colonel in the Royal Artillery, learnt from some of his officer friends that Britain was woefully unprepared against aerial attack. He arranged for his deputy ,in the Nuffield Organisation, to go to Sweden and negotiate an agreement with the Bofors Armaments people. The Chamberlain government was not interested at first, but when the gun was brought over and demonstrated to the War Office the authorities were at last impressed and they placed an order - for five Bofors guns a week.

Machine Gun Factory

In March1938,the Coventry house of Nuffield Mechanisations opened up. The building itself was then partly occupied by the engines branch of Morris Motors who were gradually moving to new, specially built, premises in another part of the town. The old buildings, hemmed in by ancient dwelling houses has a history of gun making, and the French Hotchkiss machine-gun had been made there for the 'Tommies' in World War 1. After many internal difficulties, production of the Bofors Gun commenced. As building methods in the Swedish factory at that time were very slow, modern methods of production were adopted to speed things up. In due course the personnel increased from 20 to 2,500 and the weekly output increased from 5 to 50 guns. The first Coventry made Bofors gun was delivered to the Army on the 15th June, 1939, less than 3 months before the outbreak of war! After seeing action in Norway early in the war, the evacuating British forces ditched them in the sea rather than let them fall into enemy hands. This became the fate of the first batch of Bofors guns.

photo courtesy of Coventry Museum

The Old Hotchkiss Works, Gosford Street, Coventry

Curtain of Steel

The Bofors gun then saw action in all theatres of war, some were converted to combat static guns for fitting to merchant ships to help combat the 'U' boat menace, some were used on Malta and Gibralter to combat the incessant air attacks, others to equip Dutch destroyers and cruisers of the far-eastern fleet after the Japanese invasion of the East Indies, and they were placed all around the British coast to provide a 'curtain of steel' through which the enemy had to fly to reach its target and to combat the V1 flying bomb menace late in the war.

On 'D' Day, and soon after, hundreds of Bofors guns were landed in Normandy, both towed-type and the self-propelled type, fitted to the Nuffield Organisation's own Morris Commercial four-wheel drive lorries. Many of these landed from the landing-craft on the beaches, many more came two at a time in gliders. They were also used on U.S. navy ships in the Pacific to help combat the Japanise 'Kamikaze' suicide aircraft attacks. Such was the versatility of the Bofors gun.

Air Raid

During the night of the 14th and 15th November 1940, when German bombers devastated Coventry, apart from the cathedral, the Bofors factory received four direct hits. Three high explosive bombs penetrated the roof and exploded on the concrete floor below, fortunately without doing vital damage. The fourth penetrated to the ground floor and buried itself, unnoticed, among the precious 'Barrel' machines. Fortunately, it was a dud. Had it not been, the enemy would have scored a major victory. The rifling machines were irreplaceable. The Bofors design,being Swedish (who w ere of course neutral during the war) could not be copied by the allies, nor could new machines be obtained from Sweden. We would have been sunk. So, with much haste, the decision was taken to move the precious 'rifling machines, at least, to more secluded quarters.

A fifteen-acre site was chosen near Oxford,in a dense pinewood known locally as Tubney Wood.

This was the beginning of the 'Hush-Hush' Factory.

Map of Site

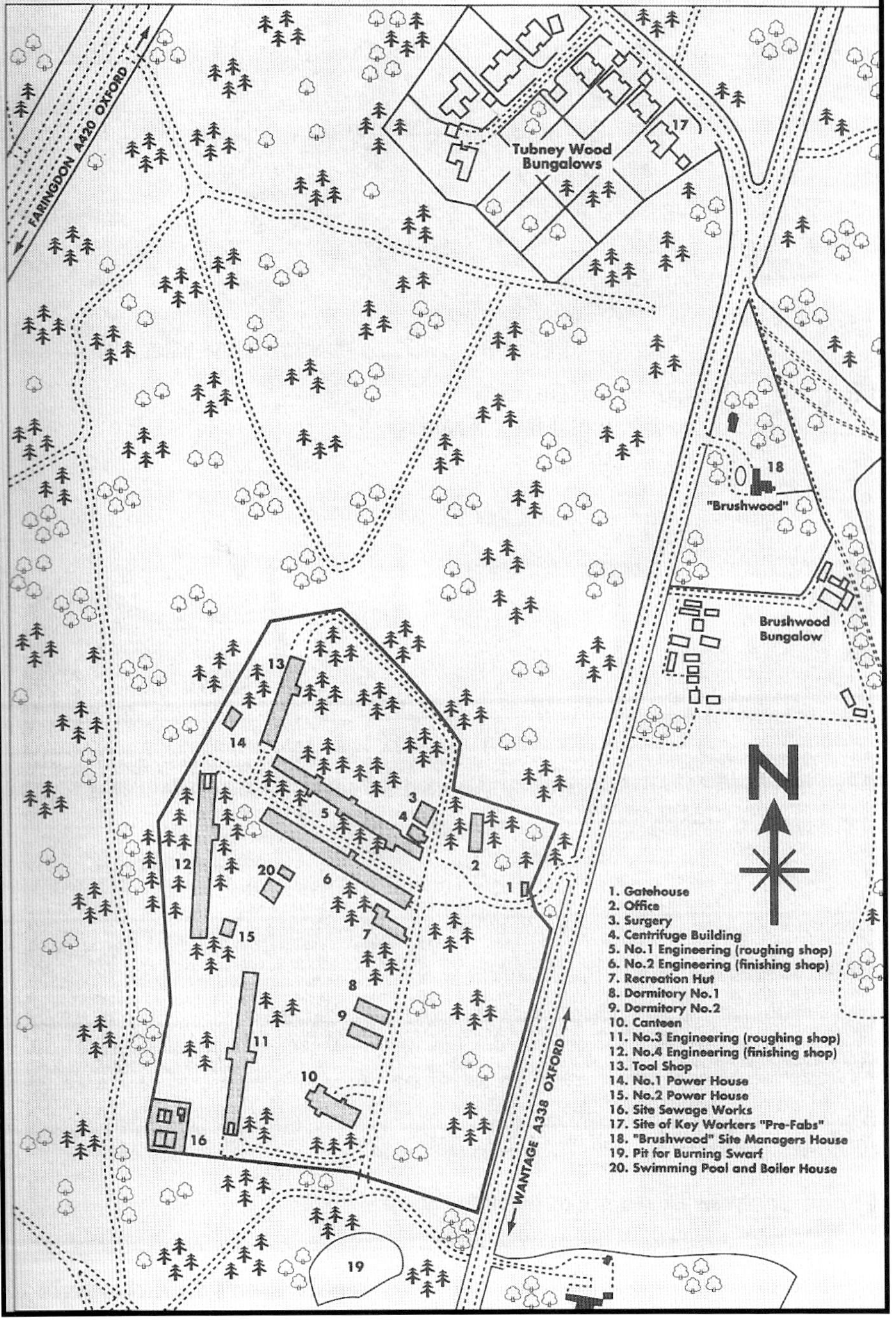

FARINGDON A420 OXFORD
Tubney Wood Bungalows
"Brushwood"
Brushwood Bungalow
WANTAGE A338 OXFORD
N
1. Gatehouse
2. Office
3. Surgery
4. Centrifuge Building
5. No.1 Engineering (roughing shop)
6. No.2 Engineering (finishing shop)
7. Recreation Hut
8. Dormitory No.1
9. Dormitory No.2
10. Canteen
11. No.3 Engineering (roughing shop)
12. No.4 Engineering (finishing shop)
13. Tool Shop
14. No.1 Power House
15. No.2 Power House
16. Site Sewage Works
17. Site of Key Workers "Pre-Fabs"
18. "Brushwood" Site Managers House
19. Pit for Burning Swarf
20. Swimming Pool and Boiler House

Part Two
The Tubney Wood Site

Blast-proof buildings concealed in the wood

An almost concealed entrance played its part in not advertising the existence of this little factory. The way the site merged with the landscape can still be seen in this 1990 photograph.

The view from just inside the gate showing the parking area with the factory buildings crouching under the trees in the background. The doors would definitely not have been painted white during the war.

The Main Factory Buildings

No.1 Engineering Shop

No.2 Engineering Shop

The Main Factory Buildings

No.3 Engineering Shop

No.4 Engineering Shop (rear view)

No.1 Powerhouse

The Factory Buildings

In 1940 work started in the wood. The builders, the local firm of Benfield and Loxley, had completed shops 1 and 2 by April 1941. It must have been difficult, with the labour and materials shortages, but they had done a superb job. Shops 1 and 2 were each 300ft long, 30ft wide and 15ft high. No.1 Shop was 30ft high at the front to accommodate the gantries for unloading the 'rough' castings that came down from Sheffield. The precious 'rifling' machines were installed in that same month and work began on the Tubney barrels.

Shops No 3 and 4 were soon built to the same dimensions, and a 200ft long Tool Shop was erected. Hill Upton and Co. Electrical and Mechanical Engineers of George Street, Oxford completed all the electrical installations, and fitted out the two power houses which together ran the whole site, but in the event of one sub-station breaking down, or being knocked out, the whole site could be run from the other, such was their capacity.

No.2 Powerhouse

Centrifuge Hut

A corrugated iron shed was built next to No.1 Shop to house the centrifuge, for removing the oil from the swarf. The oil was reclaimed and the swarf was then burnt in a pit to remove all the remaining traces of oil. The swarf was then sent away for scrap and re-processing. Good quality steel was in short supply in those dark days.

Equipment

Heating in the workshops was by 15kw fan heaters, approx 12 per shop. Lighting was provided by 125 watt 'OSIRA' lamps, the first fluorescent lamps (in bulb not strip form) approx 24 per shop. The drilling machines that did the first 'boring' of the barrels, were supplied by the Barnes Drill Co. of Rockford, Illinois, USA. Grace drilling machines were also used. Lumsden Grinders were installed in No.2 Shop, and most of the lathes were supplied by Cravens of Stockport, Cheshire. (See centre pages showing interior picture of the machine shop).

Blast Proof and Natural Camouflage

The brick buildings themselves were built to a blast proof construction, with concave roofs to hold water, and conifers were placed in large pots on the roofs to aid camouflage. Whilst the bricks were being laid, pine trees that were very close to the building line were tied back with ropes to other trees and released to spring back when the walls were completed. Whilst building was progressing, and after completion, aircraft were regularly flown overhead at various heights to test the camouflage. There was no provision for any air-raid shelters on the site, the blast-proof buildings being deemed enough protection except in the case of a direct hit. 'Blast-vents' were built into the walls at intervals along the length of the shops. These consisted of slatted vents set in with a very weak mortar mix to enable any blast to 'vent' itself with a minimum of structural damage to the buildings. Around 200 gun barrels a week were shipped out of Tubney. All were perfect. Mrs Hazel Johnson often got notes in her office saying Tubney Bofors barrels were 'the best'! The barrels were taken to be mounted and completed and then taken to a range near Clacton for the final test firing before being sent to the armed forces.

Wet Roof

Different tree species on roof

Inside the main gate, a brick building was erected for the essential checkers. Fred Stayte and Ernie Enoch were among the numbers of security and checking staff, for checking loads and personnel in and out of the factory.

A brick surgery was built, as obviously both minor and potentially major accidents could occur with people working heavy machinery under extreme pressure for such long hours. One young lady, with long blonde hair, nearly lost her scalp when her hair caught in a lathe. Quick action from a fellow worker hitting the stop button stopped the lathe just as her head reached the revolving shaft. Norman Wells, one of the electrical contractors still working on site at the time, hastily reversed the wires in the switch box, enabling her hair (or most of it) to be unwound. I believe she kept it tied up after that!

Wooden Huts

Four wooden huts were built, in true 'army-camp' style, all raised on brick piers. The one to the right of the main entrance was the office. Two others were orginally dormitories for essential workers' accommodation, the fourth, originally the canteen was used until a brick canteen was built when full production was under way.

The office by the main entrance

Wooden Dormitory (1)

Wooden Dormitory (2)

The Sewage Works

The site also had its own sewage works and proved to be still working perfectly when examined some fifty years later.

Home Guard

Most of the male employees were also members of the 'Home Guard' commanded by Second Lieutenant H.J.Palmer of B Unit of the First Berkshire (Abingdon) Battalion Home Guard, and No.39 Platoon of that organisation. They were required to turn out for for regular parades and drill, regardless of shift, to be ready to defend the factory, to the last man if necessary. Thankfully, this never happened but they were ready even if the officer in charge did hold the bullets for the rifles!

They were disbanded in August 1944.

'Consol' personnel shelter as described in the May 1939 issue of 'Popular Mechanics' magazine. The Tubney shelter has additional viewing slits for fire watching purposes.

ULAR MECHANICS 645

Portable Steel Air-Raid Shelter Has Room for Four Persons

Air-raid shelter standing under collapsing wall in severe test simulating war conditions remained undamaged from shock

Britain's drive for air-raid precautions has brought forth the development of a bell-shaped steel shell able to withstand the shock of falling bricks or shrapnel. Four people can occupy one of the shelters and come out unscathed even if a wall

Fit for a King! Advertised in the Daily Telegraph newspaper on September 4th 1939. The Tubney Wood Factory 'Consol' shelter is now preserved and being restored by the author.

The Consul /Fire-watcher's Shelter in 1992 left in situ on the roof. It has now been restored and the door secured.

The Consol Shelter

A Consol personnel shelter was placed on the roof of No.2 Shop, to be used as a fire-watcher's shelter and look-out post. The complete site was visible from this. Apart from the door hinge pins which had rusted through, so enabling the door to fall off, the shelter was in good condition (1992) and after some minor restoration and a good coat of paint it would be ready for another 50 years of standing guard.

The original wooden slatted floor and seats had rotted but could be replaced. However, it cannot have been the most sought-after job, sitting there for several hours at a time on a frosty January night!

The Shelter seen from the ground keeping its solitary watch over the woods.

The Swimming Pool

Swimming Pool

To aid recreation on site, a swimming pool was built complete with its own brick boiler house. It was of course, also the static water tank in case of fire, but was a nice thoughtful touch for the workers' enjoyment during lunch breaks and off-duty periods.

Also in 1990 a number of fire-beaters still existed, still hanging in their frames. Each consisting of a metal pipe handle, with canvas beater, the frames having pitched steel covers over them to keep them dry and all painted red. There were also other red painted cupboards dotted around the site containing hose reels and buckets with 'Fire Apparatus' painted in white across the doors.

The original fire-beaters hanging in their frames *Restored Beater*

Side view of No.2 Shop showing corrugated iron roofed bike shed

Polsten Cannons

Before the end of hostilities, when the need for Bofors guns was not so urgent, and the allies were pushing their way to the heart of Germany, Polsten cannons were produced for a short period of time, in small quantities. Then, with most of the staff having moved to other work in the area - like aero engine production at MGs in Abingdon, or the RAF Stores at Milton, the machinery that had produced so many Bofors barrels, to be used all over the world, was finally moved out. Four hectic years of production were over and so was the war.Not one bomb had fallen anywhere near the Hush-Hush factory, so good was the camouflage in that ancient wood.

The 200ft long No.5 Tool Shop, where the maintenance staff resided. See drawing opposite for locations and staff members.

Tool Shop. aka No.5. Shop

1. Electricians
2. Maintenance Crew
3. Tool Store
4. Desk
5. Tool Racks
6. Foreman
7. Side Entrance
8. Inspection Department
9. Fitters Bench
10. Fitters Bench
11. Milling Section
12. Grinding Machines
13. Toilet & Washbasins
14. Office
15. Lathes
16. Shaping Machine
17. Drills

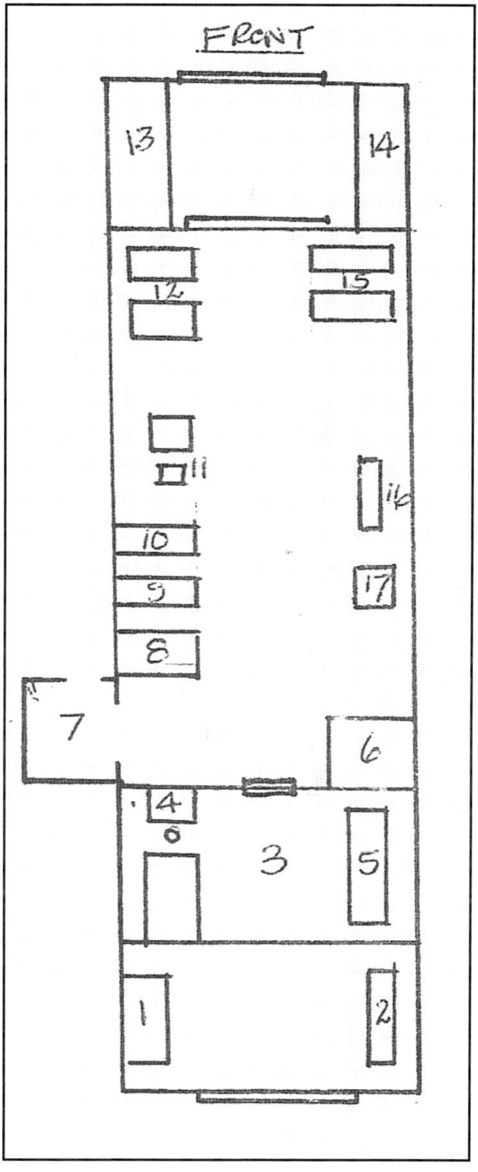

Bert Palmer was Foreman.
Other personnel consisted of :
Steve Tolan, Bert Farley, Joe Berry, Mr Partridge
All told there must have been 12 -1 5 maintenance staff

Rare period photograph of the Interior of No.1 Engineering Shop at the Hush-Hush Factory

Full of detail it is worth studying. On the right, an Inspector is checking the machined bores of the 'rough' finished barrels before they are transported to the finishing shop. The man with his arm in a sling is understood to be Mr Holmes, the factory manager, his broken arm the result of a tumble into a cable trench in the dark.

One of the blast vents can be seen above the ladies heads by the boring machines. The large press in the centre of the picture was used for stamping the details and any marks on the barrels and for truing any slight distortions that came about during machining. On the left is a double row of centre lathes which turned the outside profile of the forged billets which were delivered from Sheffield. The new 'fluorescent lamps' were the only form of lighting and the fan heaters can be seen mounted on the walls.

Small group of friends

Part Three

The Workers

Following an article in the early 90s in The Oxford Mail, a number of workers made contact with me and enabled me to write about their recollections and wonderful memories from the wartime period.

12-Hour Shifts

Mrs Rawle worked first at the munitions factory at Burghfield, near Reading. She lodged in Reading but had to move back to her home in East Hagbourne, near Didcot to look after her sick mother. She transferred to Tubney in 1943 so she could still live at home. She used to cycle from East Hagbourne to Abingdon station where she would catch the bus to the factory, then, after a 12-hour shift would do the same to return home. This was 7 days a week, summer and winter, night and day. Mrs Rawle left in 1944 after 12 months and transferred to the RAF Stores at Milton, which was much nearer to her home and where she worked on soldering and repairing aircraft radios. She continued to live in East Hagbourne.

Accommodation

Mrs Porter's late husband was an engineer at Tubney from day one, lived in temporary accommodation at the Three Horseshoes pub in Appleton, until accommodation could be provided on site. Before this he stayed in a wooden hut behind The Plough public house in Appleton. Ted Porter had worked for Nuffield Mechanisations in Coventry and moved to Tubney in 1941. After the 'Prefabs' had been built, in what is now The Ride, about half a mile from the factory, he and his wife moved into one of these. All their children were born in the prefabs.

Mrs Porter can remember the time when Canadian soldiers moved into the woods one night, on exercise, to camp there for a short while under canvas. Mrs Porter is not sure of the dates, but I am sure it was during the Excercise SPARTAN, in early March 1943. Sixteen prefabs were built and were demolished around 1978 when the site was used for new quality homes.

New Friends and Colleagues

Judy Talbot, of New Milton, near Bournemouth, Hants, worked at Tubney and kindly sent the photograph below of some of her fellow workers and herself taken in the woods during a dinner break. Edna Wooldridge, of Curbridge, near Witney, was one of the first inspectors when the factory opened in 1941, when only Nos. 1 and 2 Shops were operating. She watched Nos. 3 and 4 Shops being built and left in 1944 after illness.

Judy Talbot and friends enjoy a lunchtime break in the Tubney Woods. Mrs Bennett and Judy Talbot can be seen in the centre of the front row and Mrs Gray is 2nd from left on the back row.

Mrs Dinah Arnold then Miss Dinah Wells, a seventeen and a half year old from Marcham, operated a lathe in No.2 Shop. She remembered that Tubney was always referred to as the 'Hush-Hush' factory. She later transferred to MGs at Abingdon.

Mrs M.G.Bennett worked for several years in No.2 Shop, both day and night shifts , fortnights about, until ill health forced her to leave. She later went to live in Cumnor Village.

Mrs Iris Duckworth, then Iris Day, worked for two years at Tubney until the site closed at the end of the war and then transferred to MGs at Abingdon. She later moved to Chorley, Lancs.
(There is further reference to Iris later).

Mrs Vera Bisp, then Vera Parrott of Southmoor, near Abingdon worked in No.1 shop as a lathe operator from 1941 to 1944.

Mrs Hazel Johnson, widow of Albert Johnson (Appleton) worked in the office from 1942 to 1944.

Family of Workers

Mrs Mabel Sharpe of Witney, then Miss McKenzie was bussed in from Faringdon and started work in No.1 Shop soon after the factory opened. However, not long into her new employment she injured a finger badly in one of the machines, she was taken to hospital and then had to have two months off work recovering. When she returned it was on a boring machine in No.2 Shop where, due to the cutting oil had to wear overalls and clogs but even so still enjoyed it. She remembers having her dinners in the canteen, listening to 'Workers Playtime'. Mrs Sharpe's mother and sister also worked at Tubney but Mrs Sharpe was there the longest. She was employed for three years, day and night shifts until the Faringdon bus stopped running and she was forced to leave.
Like so many others she then went to work at the MG car factory at Abingdon. She had very fond memories of the Hush-Hush factory and the friends she made there. It is possible that she is shown in one of the period photos.

Walking Wounded

June Bloomfield, then Miss Cobb, started work in the late spring of 1942 after working in the service of Sir Kenneth and Lady Nicholson of Fyfield Manor. Mrs Bloomfield worked on No.1 shop on a lathe, boring the rough barrels and completing other initial processess. She well remembers the time her friend Daisy's jumper caught on the rough surface of the revolving barrel which threw her right over the lathe and nearly severed her thumb. June was then asked to accompany Daisy to the Radcliffe Infirmary in Oxford. They both walked from Tubney to hospital to get the thumb stitched, at night, in thick fog. On reaching Botley they asked a policeman if they were going in the right direction, and the policeman replied "I think so, but I've just about lost myself in this fog!". The next morning they did manage to hitch a lift back to Tubney so they could clock-off.

She also vividly remembers a man named Joe who worked the overhead gantry moving six barrels at a time in a 'sling'. The barrels slipped, crushing his hand severely in the process. June remembers how sad they all were as Joe's wife had just given birth to twins. As the National Health Service did not exist at the time, being unable to work he was unfortunately devoid of any income.

Mrs Bloomfield remembers well the day in the summer of 1942 when a Bofors gun was demonstrated to the Tubney staff one lunchtime by members of the Royal Artillery. She recalls how disappointed they were when the officer said, "Of course, we won't actually be able to fire it." Nevertheless, it was nice for them to know what they were toiling long and hard for, and to see the finished product. Mrs Bloomfield finished at Tubney late in 1944 and after helping with the Polsten Cannon production, which she says was very difficult, as the drills, which were half the diameter of the Bofors, kept breaking inside the Polsten Barrels.

She then transferred to MGs at Abingdon where she was a riveter on Tempest aircraft wings, a job she loved as it was really interesting after the very heavy repetitious work at Tubney. After the war she moved back to Tubney and worked in the surgical stores. She later went to live in the Southampton area.

Group of happy workers enjoying their break

More lovely ladies showing snoods/ turbans to keep their hair in place

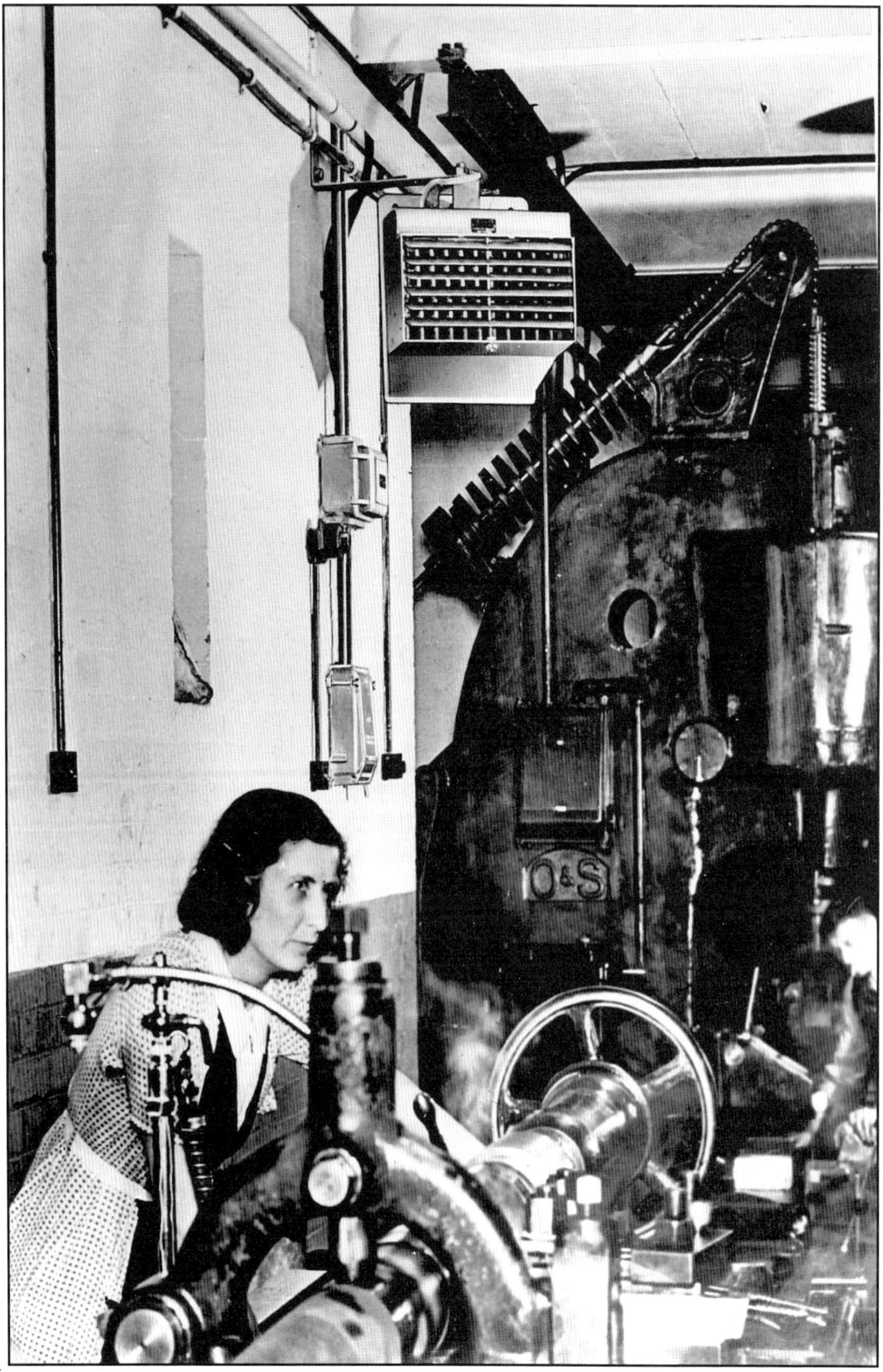
O&S

Working the Lathe

Mrs Lilian Coleman, known as Kitty to her friends, is the lady in the picture working her lathe at Tubney. Her photo was featured in an Oxford Mail article by Don Chapman and her son and two daughters got a pleasant surprise to see her. All have confirmed her identity to me. It was originally thought by Mr Norman Wells (the electrician) that she was an evacuee from London and it is indeed true that she and her family did move from Acton in London to Oxford. Mrs Coleman also had an accident involving the lathe and was taken by car to hospital. After convalescing she returned to become manageress of the canteen. She apparently bore the scars of her lathe accident for the rest of her life. Her son and one daughter live in Oxford whilst another daughter lives in Paignton, Devon.

This photo shows the position of the lathe next to the press alcove.

This is the alcove where the press stands in the photo showing Kitty. She is working the lathe that stands next to it.

Young Starter

Mr Roy Collett from Grove, near Wantage was, without doubt the youngest member of the Tubney staff. He lived in Wootton Rd, Abingdon next to **Mr R Chester** who was a fireman at Tubney. On leaving Boxhill school, Mr Chester took him along to see Mr Holmes the manager. The only job available for a fourteen year old youngster was in the tool stores of No.5 shop. Along with most local people he cycled in daily. There were two storemen who worked alternate days and nights, **Mr Fred Ridge and Mr Bill Hunter.** The job was to issue the large assortment of tools required in the machine shops. The girls used to bring them back for re-sharpening in the tool shop, fresh ones were given in exchange. Once a week a lorry would arrive from Gosford St with mundane items such as light bulbs, toilet rolls, cleaning cloths and medical supplies. One of Roy's duties was to deliver the stores items around the various buildings, apparently running the gauntlet of all the young ladies, with much blushing on his part! He was fascinated by the machine tools and eventually plucked up courage to ask for a transfer to the tool room. He was taken under **Steve Tolan's** wing who taught Roy the basics of milling practice. Any spare moments in the tool shops were used for making cigarette lighters as matches were very scarce at that time. Being the youngest and least vital to operations he tended to be the errand-boy and every morning would go round the shop and take orders for cigarettes. He then delivered his orders to a lady in the canteen through a little cubby hole. Roy also remembers the Bofors gun-crew arriving and performing a barrel change in front of all the staff. They must have thought their luck had changed performing in front of so many pretty young girls! He also remembers the weekly ENSA concert party and an occasional film show in the canteen. He recalls that despite the shortages of war the canteen food, although plain was plentiful and well cooked, ideal for a growing lad!

In 1943 Roy left Tubney and went to Wellworthy Piston Rings in the temporary works of the Pavlova Leather Company where pistons for aircraft engines were being manufactured. National Service and an apprenticeship followed, then Roy joined AERE Harwell for the rest of his working life. He enjoyed his time at Tubney. He has drawn the diagram of the tool shop interior from memory.

Machinist in No.1 Shop

Mrs. Gray of Freeland, near Witney,then Miss Winifred Baston is shown on the group photo. The original photo caption failed to name her but that mystery is now solved. She first lived near Newbridge, then moved to Appleton which wasn't so far to cycle on a cold winters night. She worked at Tubney as a machinist in No.1 Shop from its opening. The foreman of the shop was Mr Albert Johnson and she worked for him boring the barrels on both day and night shifts. Towards the end of production she moved to the office attached to No.4 Shop.

She recalls the Rozalex barrier cream the operatives were supposed to use and always enjoyed the ENSA troop performances.
She remembers with much affection the beautiful bluebells and wild flowers in the spring and the scent of the pines and the nightingales singing during the midnight to 1am meal breaks in the summer months.
Mrs Gray transferred to MGs in August 1944 at the end of production working in the material control office. At the time MGs were making Rolls Royce Merlin engines for Lancaster bombers.

The ENSA wall art of Roosevelt, Churchill and Stalin was drawn in charcoal on one of the insulation panels in the original canteen.

Sylvia and Ben Malpas met in the canteen during one of Ben's frequent deliveries of stores from Coventry to Tubney.

Ben drove a petrol Fordson 7V lorry during this period (as pic)

Other Employees

Mr and Mrs Tolan of Marcham. Mr Tolan was an engineer and met his wife at the factory. Mrs Tolan stayed on as stated previously, as supervisor of the medical equipment store. Mr Tolan went to MGs to work on the 'Neptune' amphibian project and then the aero engines. Following that he worked at Harwell. Mrs Sylvia Malpas, then Miss Smith, worked in both canteens and met her late husband Ben there. Ben was a delivery driver delivering materials and machinery from Coventry to Tubney. Mrs Malpas lived in Marcham.
Margaret Begg remembered one night when the bus from Oxford broke down, a truck turned up to transport them into work. The girls sang 'Deep in the heart of Texas' all the way in! She worked there for two years.

Mr Hancock was the first factory manager, soon to be replaced by a Mr Holmes, lived at 'Brushwood' a large house still in existence almost opposite the factory gates. The Chief Fire Officer was Mr Archie Scott and a Swede by the name of Hans Lansart, who was an engineer on site lived at Boars Hill. It is believed his daughters still live in the area.

Historic Photographs

Norman Wells, mentioned previously of Shipton-on-Cherwell worked for Hill Upton and Co. the electrical contractors on site as an electrician and helped to install all the wiring, switchboxes, lights and heaters.

He left after No.1 and 2 Shops were in production but saw the start of Nos. 3 and 4 being built. He obtained two superb photographs offcially taken for Hill Upton of the interior of No. 1 Shop.
When Hill Upton were taken over the offices were cleared of all paper work, records and photographs. Luckily Mr Wells managed to rescue two for old times' sake and together with Mrs Talbot's are, to my knowledge the only period photos that are available of the Hush-Hush factory at Tubney.
Sidney Watson and Fred Whitlock both worked for Pressed Steel at Tubney after the war making mock-ups for new car bodywork. Mr Watson went to live in Grimsby and Mr Whitlock to Eynsham.

News in 2013

In November 2013 I received a phone call from Mr Andrew Mansell and he subsequently wrote to me.
This is an extract from his letter

Please find enclosed my late mother-in-law's (Iris Duckworth, nee Day) notebook from her days working in the inspection department at the Bofors gun barrel factory in Tubney Woods during WW2.
We found a copy of your book that was sent to her 20 years ago, on her 70th birthday from her friend Judy Talbot along with covering letter and newspaper clipping. Luckily we found your book and the letter first as we later found Iris's notebook in the loft and realised its significance.
Iris was an only child from quite a religious (Salvation Army) family and lived with her parents in Victoria Rd, so the thought of her working in a factory must have been quite daunting as a young girl at that time.
In fact they said she was 'like a fish out of water' at first, but she soon overcame that and got on with the vital job at hand. Iris made many life-long friends working at Tubney and said she really enjoyed her time there, but not so much at MG when she transferred.

Iris met her husband at this time, Alan Duckworth from Chorley, Lancs. He was serving in the RAF stationed at Abingdon, she said that Alan would bike with her to the Tubney Woods factory whenever he could. The couple later got married and had their only child Julie, in 1952. They later moved back to Alan's home town where Iris lived until her death in 2010, Alan had passed away in 1996.

After so many intervening years it was quite a surprise to be sent Iris's notebook which she had kept all those years.
Thank you to Andrew and Julie Mansell for saving this small bit of history from Tubney.

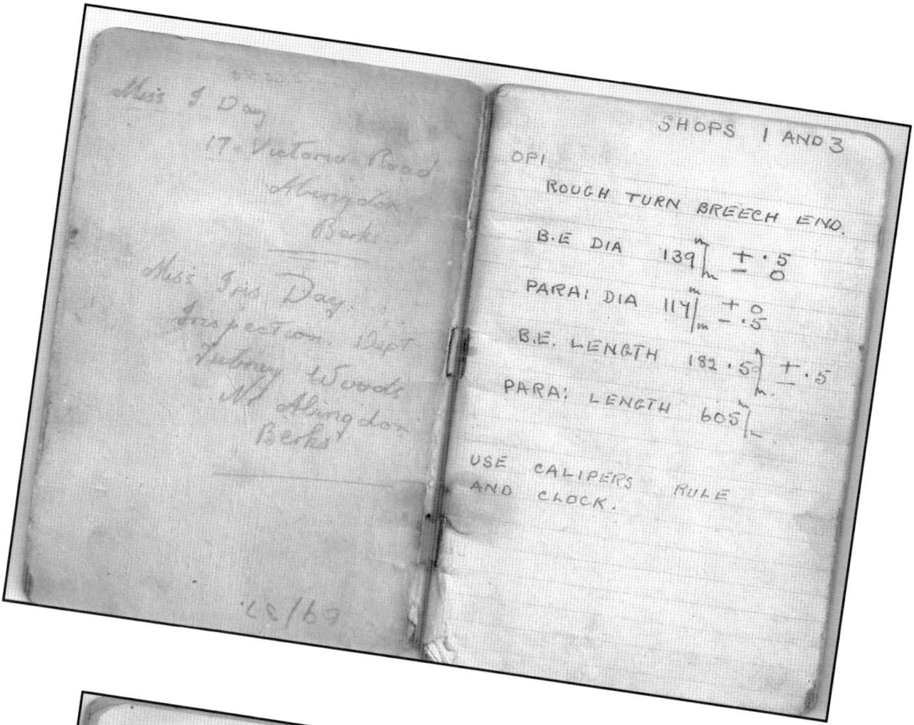
Miss I Day
17 Victoria Road
Abingdon
Berks

Miss Iris Day
Inspection Dept
Tubney Woods
Nr Abingdon
Berks

SHOPS 1 AND 3
OP1
ROUGH TURN BREECH END.
B.E DIA 139 m/m +.5 −0
PARA: DIA 114 m/m +0 −.5
B.E. LENGTH 182.5 m/m ±.5
PARA: LENGTH 605 m/m
USE CALIPERS RULE
AND CLOCK.

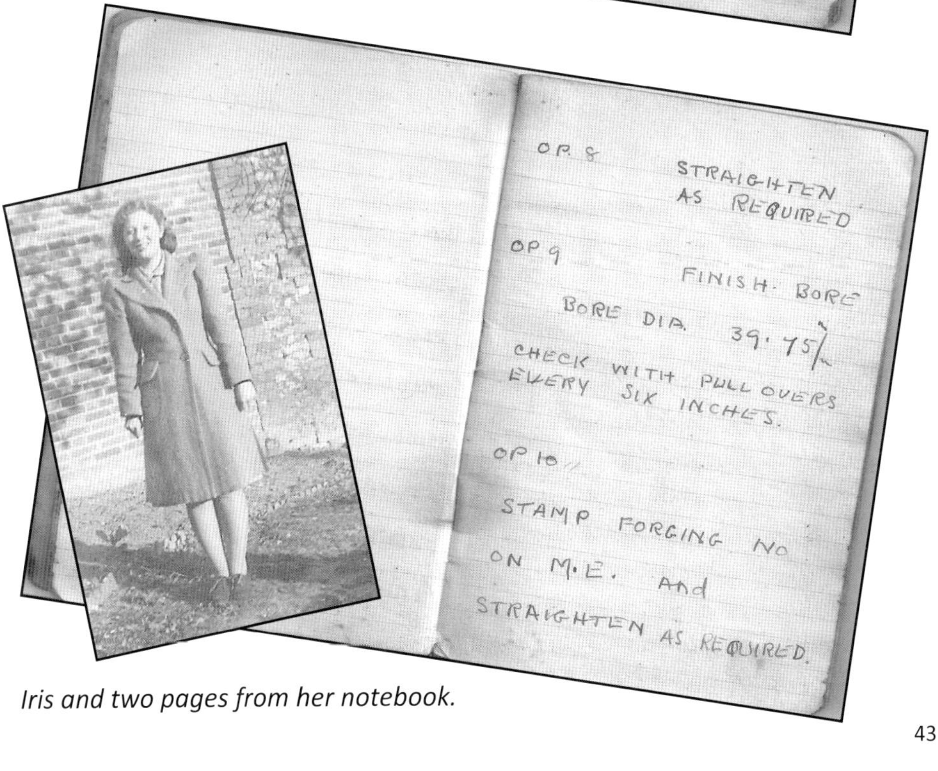
OP. 8 STRAIGHTEN
AS REQUIRED
OP 9
FINISH BORE
BORE DIA. 39.75 m/m
CHECK WITH PULL OVERS
EVERY SIX INCHES.
OP 10
STAMP FORGING NO
ON M.E. And
STRAIGHTEN AS REQUIRED.

Iris and two pages from her notebook.

Part Four

Post War and Survival

From Surgical Stores to Double Glazing

After the war these huge, solid buildings were used by the Ministry of Supply to store surgical items.

Everything from face masks and gowns to complete surgical theatres. Overproduction of these items and now the lack of casualties to use them meant they had to be stored somewhere until they could be put to good use. What better place than Tubney. Mrs Tolan from Marcham was the supervisor of the Medical Equipment Store. Appropriately, her office was in the old site surgery.

When the Ministry of Supply moved out, Pressed Steel moved in. The buildings were then used for the making of mock-up car bodies for the post-war car industry. They then continued to use the buildings for the storage of their 'Prescold' fridges. Prescold was a British refridgeration manufacturer established by the Pressed Steel Co.Ltd of Oxford in 1934. They were often known for their good design and durability. The fridge business went sour with the advent of cheap imports, mainly from Italy, the fridge capital of the world.

So, in the sixties, Tubney was at last cleared, but not for good.

The Hill Upton Switchgear and sign on the equipment

Trading Estate

With the ever-growing problem of the third world countries Oxfam was formed and once again the old buildings were brought back from the brink. This time being used for the storage of blankets, clothes and other items destined for those under privileged countries. The main contractor for Oxfam moved his HQ and transport fleet to Tubney, and gradually the site became of trading estate status. Mr M Miles, a specialist welder, moved into No.1 sub-station and Mr G Mitchell took over No.3 workshop for the spraying of commercial vehicles,the company being known as HGV Services until he moved to Milton Trading Estate at Didcot.

Inside of No.2 Shop showing the length of the building,ideal for storage.

Brick Canteen.

A final sight of the interior of the centrifuge shed - above shows the oil container in the floor and left the gantry on the ceiling

Later Years

In later years most of the buildings were rented by R.M.Johnson, who used some of the buildings for the storage of their plastic products, including thousands of road cones, dustbins and buckets. Two of the buildings were sub-let to Peter Geekie Ltd, who stored swimming pool equipment there. Rokold, the refridgerated transport specialist had their office in one of the wooden huts.
Defra Design were another company located there, with draughtsmen preparing design drawings for Oxford Instruments, and B. J. Johnson, double glazing manufacturers who occupied the brick canteen buildings as their office and workshop.

All subsequently moved out when the site was sold by Magdalen College in Oxford to the Newbury developers Sedgebrook PLC in 1989. Sedgebrook bought the site for development, the college's description being somewhat suspect, referring to the site as 'derelict'. When it was sold, all buildings were occupied. Magdalen College was still demanding rent for the 'derelict' buildings and the Vale of White Horse Council was still receiving rates! No mention of its historical past was made by the college to Sedgebrook.

Preservation

In 1987, I wrote to the Department of the Environment asking for them to consider listing the site because of its historical past. The reply came back that 'after inspection by the English Heritage experts, because none of the original equipment existed inside, they did not deem the buildings to be of architectural or historical interest'.
I was not happy with that, so contacted my local MP Mr John Patten, who wrote to the then Under Secretary for the Environment Mrs Virginia Bottomley. The reply came back agreeing with English Heritage, so sadly I had done all I could.

The fate of the gun factory site at Tubney was sealed.

It was to be demolished!

Magazine Article

At the time of writing to the D.o.E. I also contacted *After The Battle* magazine who already knew of the site's existance. They had visited it about 10 years previously and had photographed the then unoccupied site without knowing what had been the original purpose. They had removed an interior panel from one of the wooden huts, on which was a charcoal drawing of Stalin, Roosevelt and Churchill, with the caption 'Keep smiling, it won't be long now!'. It had been drawn by a member of ENSA (The Entertainment National Service Association) who had provided concerts in the canteen during the war years, and was initialled L.A.C. and dated 16/4/42.

After the Battle ran an article in issue 62, August 1988, with facts supplied by myself and a report written by John Steane, then of Oxfordshire Museum at Woodstock after I had contacted them. They had not heard of the site and John Steane carried out the investigation. He had managed to locate and interview Mr Albert Johnson, now deceased, the foreman and second in command of the factory during the war. His memories were a valuable source of information with regard to the happenings at Tubney. I also contacted Don Chapman who at that time was a writer for our local newspaper, The Oxford Mail, he then published a piece in the paper using the information I had collected. In this article he asked for any former workers to contact me. A number did, from as far afield as Grimsby, Lancashire and Bournemouth as well as the local people. Their stories are recorded in the earlier section on the workers.

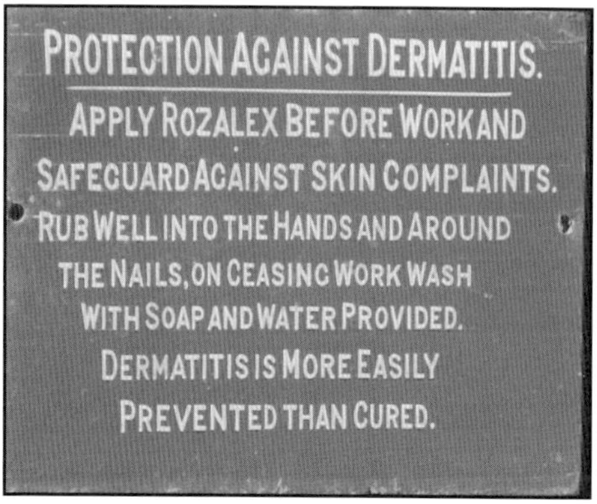

Saved from the factory - the Rozalex sign and a green lampshade

Part Five
Demolition

Sights set on former gun factory land

OXFORD Instruments wants to build a massive new complex on the historic site of a wartime gun factory at Tubney Woods.

The 15-acre site in the middle of the woods, near Abingdon, produced giant Bofors guns in the war, but was demolished after Newbury developers Sedgebrook bought it in 1987.

Now it is the chosen site for a proposed relocation of Oxford Instruments' nuclear magnetic resonance division from Osney Mead in Oxford.

Oxford Instruments is understood to agreed terms on a £1.75m deal to buy the land.

It has applied to the Vale of White Horse District Council for planning permission for a 79,000 sq ft office, research and manufacturing headquarters for the NMR division, which makes huge superconducting magnets and employs about 200 people.

The outline application has the backing of Vale planning officers who are recommending that a decision to approve it be delegated to the planning and development committee chairman subject to planning agreements.

The site became a gun factory in 1940 when the War Ministry built a self-contained camp with its own surgery and swimming pool in the middle of chose medieval wood.

Production of 40mm Bofors guns, developed in Sweden, went on around the clock at the works, which was a closely guarded secret never discovered by Hitler's bombers.

Magdalen College, Oxford sold the land to Sedgebrook in 1987 and the buildings were demolished in 1983 after two invasions by New Age Travellers and an attempt to hold a rave party there scuppered a campaign for the site to be listed because of its historic value.

Set up by Sir Martin Wood in 1959, Oxford Instruments is now a £163m multinational group.

It made profits of £12.8m on a turnover of £112m last year, exports 85 per cent of its products and employs 1,200 staff in Oxfordshire.

A report to today's meeting of the planning committee, says: "Although a single building is now proposed rather than the permitted three separate buildings, the proposal is for a single user, it complies with the restrictions imposed on the existent permission, it ensures the site is developed in accordance with the Local Plan's requirements and it would enable the desired relocation of a prestigious local company."

Newspaper headline announces the site for sale.
Oxford Mail March 1995

Preservation

It is a great pity that bodies like the Vale of White Horse District Council and the Department of the Environment do not recognise what treasures are available to us. Whilst I appreciate that everything cannot,and perhaps should not, be saved, I do believe that every step should be taken to preserve something like Tubney. There are many people such as myself who are very interested in WW2 history and much of that era is still around in various guises and states of repair. From preserved military vehicles to pill boxes in the fields, from hundreds of books on the subject to preserved battleships and cruisers, it was invaluable that during my original research I was able to speak to a number of people who were there - be it on the battlefield or equally important, the home front.

The Rescue

In November 1990 I received a telephone call one Friday afternoon advising that the empty site was being invaded by gypsies intent on cutting up and removing anything steel for scrap. I was greatly concerned for the Consol shelter remaining on the roof of No.2 Shop, so initiated a rescue operation for the following morning. I made several telephone calls, one to Sedgebrook obtaining permission to remove the Consol, one to a farmer friend to provide a safe haven in the near vicinity, one to a friend to provide transport and I asked my then employer if I could 'borrow' his 18 ton mobile crane and operator.

Having obtained permission from them all, we met at 10am the following morning to remove the shelter from its lofty perch of 50 years. With much excitement and just a hint of sadness, the crane lowered it to the ground and we duly transported it to its new safe location. Out of hundreds made during the war, research reveals only a dozen or so left in the country, but that aside, I feel my Tubney one is special.

The crane carefully removes the CONSOL shelter from the roof

Final Days

By February 1992 the site was still defying the developers although now an invasion of 'New Age Travellers' had reduced the area into an appalling state. Steps were taken and trenches dug to prevent a repeat happening. However, after another potential 'hippie' invasion and a thwarted 'rave party' the police advised Sedgebrook that this sort of thing was bound to happen again if the buildings remained in a derelict condition. Sedgebrook decided to demolish.

On Thursday March 26th, 1992 a demolition company moved in and started the demolition process, almost exactly fifty one years since the secret Hush-Hush factory started production of Bofors Gun Barrels.

Demolition of the buildings gets under way

Various stages of the demolition

Note thickness of the blastproof wall and the blast vent double skin section

The Redeveloped site known as The Ride

The Ride (above)

Map showing position of property (right)

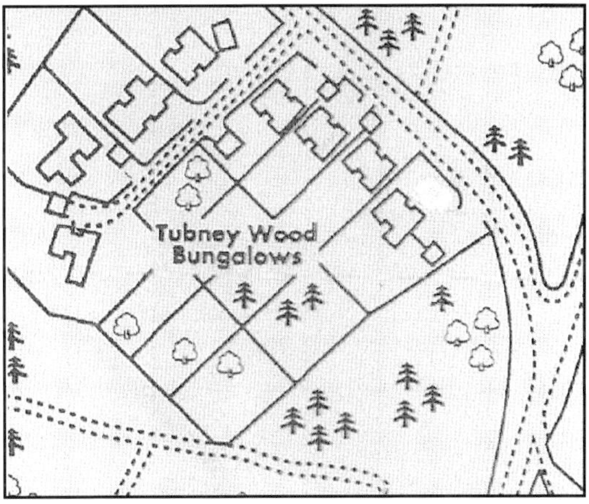

The road named 'The Ride' at Tubney Wood, just off the A338, was the spot chosen to erect the prefabs for the essential workers that came down from the Coventry factory to start up the shadow factory at Tubney Wood. Later, when the prefabs were eventually demolished it was decided that good quality houses would be built on the site. A total of eight detached properties were built in the 1980s.

New Industry for Tubney Wood

Main Entrance 2014 and inset the old gatehouse
The buildings still partially concealed from the road by the Tubney trees.

After lying dormant for a time, building work started on the new premises for Oxford Instruments plc, which is a United Kingdom manufacturing and research company that designs and manufactures tools and systems for industry and research. The company was founded in 1959 to manufacture super conducting magnets for use in scientific research.
It is gratifying to know that the former BOFORS Gun Barrel factory in Tubney Wood is still associated with precision engineering, albeit to a different scale and end use.

My Thanks
Thank you to Don chapman, formerly of *The Oxford Mail,* and Winston Ramsey of *AfterThe Battle* magazine for the coverage they provided to preserve part of our history and heritage. I am certain that without their help to publicise this matter, the site would have been demolished without trace. At least, in part through this publication, the site will be known more to the general public and I am grateful to the number of ex-staff who contacted me, so enabling me to complete my research.
My utmost thanks goes to each of them and also to everyone who has helped and encouraged in this, to me, important task.

BOFORS

Vår referens Our reference
L O Karlsson

Er referens Your reference

Vår datum Our date
August 6, 1992

Er datum Your date

Sida Page
1 (1)

Mr Nigel J Dawe
47 Elizabeth Avenue
Peachcroft Farm
Abingdon, Oxon OX14 2 NS
England

Dear Mr Dawe,

Thank you for giving us a copy of your very interesting booklet on the 40 mm gun barrel factory.

I am absolutely confident that also Terry Gander enjoyed reading it. I enclose a copy of his 40 mm book in case you have not received one.

Furthermore, I have passed your booklet and your wishes to Mr Sven Jungmarker who is in charge of "our heritage" and takes care of our museum. Please don´t hesitate to contact him if you should want to.

His address is:

Information Department
Bofors AB
S–691 80 Karlskoga
Sweden

If you by any chance make a trip to Sweden, please contact us and we will consider it a privilege to give you a personal tour in our museum.

Yours sincerely,

BOFORS AB
COMMUNICATIONS & PUBLIC AFFAIRS

Lars Olof Karlsson

Bofors is a member of the Celsius Group

Postadress Postal address
S-691 80 KARLSKOGA, Sweden

Telefon
0586-810 00
Telephone
+46 586 810 00

Telex
73210 bofors s
Telefax
0586-581 45
+46 586 581 45

Bankgiro Bank Giro No
605 30 29
Postgiro Postal Giro No
65 00-3